Just
Jimmy
Ink

JIMMY LINDSEY JR.

PAGE PUBLISHING, INC.
Conneaut Lake, PA

First originally published by Page Publishing 2021

ISBN 978-1-6624-6061-6 (pbk)
ISBN 978-1-6624-2116-7 (hc)
ISBN 978-1-6624-2115-0 (digital)

Printed in the United States of America

Poems

Homeless

He lives in a house made out of cardboard
Because he lost the home he couldn't afford
With rags 4 clothes no shoes on his feet
Looking 4 a way to make ends meet
He picks up cans out on the street
And begs 4 money so he can eat

Oh, what would it be like to be homeless
No children to hug or wife to kiss
He looks at the razor then at his wrist
How would you like to live like this
Oh, what would it be like to be homeless

He looks on the ground 4 cigarette butts
People watching him think he's nuts
A half pint of whiskey in a paper sack
He stumbles on down to the railroad track
Thinks maybe he'll stay in a boxcar tonight
The clouds are moving in there's rain insight

Wondering why God doesn't hear his prayer
Or if there's even a God up there
He bends to his knees and says father please
Help me I'm lost and all alone
Could you please, please bring me home

Imagine yourself wanting to die
Unable to cry not knowing why
You have no home and your all alone
No one to love hug or kiss
These are the things that you would miss
And that's what it's like to be homeless…

I Picture

I picture my little girl waiting by the door
When I don't come home
She waits some more
She says, "Momma!"
"Where's Daddy? He promised he'd be here."
She'll say, "Honey!"
"Maybe he just stopped to have a beer."
I picture my little girl falling down and balling
Wondering why her Daddy wasn't there to keep her from falling

CHORUS
She says to herself, "I wonder if he loves me."
"Is he thinking of me?"
"Daddy, Daddy, where have you been?"
"Why do you keep doing the same things again and again?"
"If you really loved me, you'd be a Daddy instead of my best friend."

I picture my little girl hugging her teddy bear
And I'm feeling guilty because I'm not there
I picture my little girl in a room by herself
Staring at a picture of her Daddy that sits on the shelf
I picture my little girl crying and all alone
Because I broke my promise and didn't come HOME

Dad

You coached me in football and baseball too
I wanted to win just for you
Losing was not an option for me
I wanted to be the best I could be
I found out I can't always win
But It's only a sin if you don't get back up again
You taught me never to stay down
To be the first one up off the ground
I wanted to tell you I'm still standing now
Because you're the one who taught me how
Today I don't always have the winning score
Because winnings not about the score anymore
WINNING has a new meaning where I sit
I call it never give up never quit

P.S.
Dad, when I wrote this I cried. It brought feelings out from deep inside
Love you, Dad!
From Jimmy Lindsey Jr.

Should 'ah

Should 'ah never picked up drugs and alcohol
Should 'ah never hidden behind the 8 ball
Should 'ah been stronger—should 'ah stood tall
Should 'ah did the right thing or nothing at all
Should 'ah known by the look in your eyes
Should 'ah of been focused eyes on the prize
Instead I chased women in faded Levi's
Of all the things I should 'ah done
I didn't do
I did do one
I sure loved you!
Should 'ah been a better brother and a better son
Should 'ah been a better man made you number 1
Should 'ah been a better Daddy 4 Paige Ann and Casey Lee
Should 'ah been the man Lord wanted me to be
Should 'ah kept living the night Bobby died
Something got in the way something deep down inside
I guess it's what a simple man calls foolish pride
Of all the things I should 'ah done
I didn't do
I did do one e e
I sure loved you!

Should I Pray 4 My Hands

Tell me where do I begin
How do I make amends
For a heart that's been
Broken once again
Yeah, I committed a sin
I went and did it again
Now what can I do
To make it up to you

Should I get on my knees
Should I pray for my hands
Give my hands something real
Something they can feel
Yeah give my hands something real

Lord, can you tell me why
She chose another guy
Why she made me cry
Was her love a lie
Should I give it another try
I guess I'll just get high
Until the tears run dry
Lord could you tell me why
I miss that look in her eyes
O Lord, could you tell me why

Yeah, I committed a sin
I went and did it again
I gave a girl my heart
She went and tore it apart
Tell me lord how do I mend
This broken heart once again

How do I repay you for
The pain you let me feel
Should I pray for my hands
Give my hands something real
Something that they can feel
Yeah, give my hands something real

Should I thank you for
The slap in the face
Or the bitter taste
For all the dreams erased
For the loss of her embrace
Was our love a waste
You know I miss her smile'n face

I guess I learned my lesson
No more second guessing
Should I get out my Smith and Wesson
Or take my broken heart
And give her my bless'n
I guess I'll just set her love free
If it comes back it was meant to be

Cocaine

Cocaine's always been there through all my hard times
It stood by my side when I committed my crimes
It stayed with me through my sleepless nights
Even when I was wrong, it told me I was right

Chorus

Cocaine imprisoned me
Look what it's done to me
Then come hang with me
Because misery loves company

Cocaine was there through my darkest hour
It gave me strength when I had no power
It was there when I lost my family and home
Yeah, cocaine would never leave me alone

When I needed a friend, it was always there
If I broke promises, it didn't even care
Cocaine even loved me when I was insane
It helped me bury all my guilt and shame

Cocaine was with me when life got tough
It helped me pawn off all my stuff
Cocaine always called me on my bluff
Yeah, I loved cocaine but could never get enough

When I was cry'n and begg'n for God
Oh please, please, hear my prayer
Cocaine was there
When I begged for God to care
cocaine was there

Things I Love

I love watching the Skies as the storms roll in
Listening to the thunder and watching the lightning
After the storms roll through, a rainbow will appear
Giving me the feeling that heaven is near
I love the birds and the bees
And the flowers and the trees
I love the clouds in the sky
And the deep blue seas
I love God because he gave me all of these
I love things that mesmerize
Like the seasons, the sunsets, and the sunrise
I love the angels in heaven and eternity
Because these are the things God has promised me

Wild Heart

I think I know what's wrong with me
I'm a little wild and I want to be free
I know in my heart
I've been this way from the start
Always looking for a battle to figh
Even though I'm not always right
Because I've been this way for so long
I don't feel like I'm doing nothing wrong
Well I don't think I can go back to start
And change all the things that are in my heart
Because even when I was a child
I loved being free and running wild
So take away the fence and the bars
Give me the moon and the stars
So I can go to a place I've never been
And be WILD AT HEART once again
There's one thing I know for sure
I love my life it's an adventure
Taking chances and being brave
Or looking for a princess I can save
I don't like being tied down
Or having my face pushed on the ground
MY FREEDOM MEANS A LOT
BUT A WILD HEART IS WHAT I GOT

Best Friends

The night Bobby died
The night we all cried
Scattered pieces everywhere
I've been to hell and back
But you're not there

So you're in a better place now
I still see you somehow
Cause that's what best friends do
They never really leave you
Yeah they are there till the end
Cause they're your best friend

So if I don't find you
Down here in this hell
Save me a room at the same hotel
And when I check in
I'll say I'm look'n
For my best friend
I'll find you whole again
And you'll be the same
As you were back then
You'll be my best friend

I can't believe that our days are done
But if it's TRUE that only the good die young
Then Bobby was the chosen one

Fill the Hole

I cried and I cried then I tried
To hide my wounds deep inside
I smiled to hide my fears
Turned my face to hide my tears

Chorus

The devil took my heart
Took my soul...
took my life
Yeah, he took control
Then he left a hole

My demons took me straight to hell
The more I struggled, the farther I fell
He started by taking little things
Then he took what heaven brings
Took my house, took my home
Still wouldn't leave me alone
Took my kids, took my wife
Now he wants to take my life
Go on devil!

Now I'm digg'n deep bringing feelings out
That's what changing your life is all about
I found my heart in recovery
It's been my greatest discovery
I had to cast out the bad in me
To be the best I could be

I said, "Lord, take my heart, take my soul,"
"Take my life, yeah, take control,"
"And fill the hole,"
"Yeah, fill the hole."

Teddy Bear

Well I came home late again
Rocky says, "Jimmy, where you been?"
I look her straight in the eyes
start telling the same old lies?

She was shaking her head
At every word I said
There was nothing she was buying
She said, "Dammit, Jimmy, you're a lie'n."

But my daughter who was standing there
Said, "Uh-uh, Momma, Daddy's not a lion, he's a teddy bear."
"And, Momma! When you say Daddy's a lion, it just isn't fair,"
"See? I know Daddy's a teddy bear."

Yeah, I know Daddy's a teddy bear
Because I can take him by the hand and drag him anywhere.
And when my belly hurts, I can hug him tight
And in just a little while everything's alright
I can take my bear with me when I go beddy-bye
he's a comfort to me if I start to cry
Yeah, I love just cuddling with my teddy bear
Things aren't the same when he's not there
See, Momma? Daddy's not a lion, he's a teddy bear

One Love

When I think about love, I think about you
Some say one and one makes two
But not when it comes to me and you
I respect everything you try to do
When you're hurting, I cry for you
If you need me, I'd die for you
That's why we're one—not two

Cause it's ONE LOVE that can't be broke
ONE LOVE that can't be stole
ONE LOVE that makes us whole
That's why unconditional's all about
Loving you, baby, from the inside out

I loved you at first sight
I loved you with all my might
And loving you, baby, feels so right
You open up the heavens at night
Without you, I wouldn't know what to do
That's why we're one, not two

God made you just for me
I'm going to love you till eternity
You're the one who sets my heart free
And you make the fire burn in me
That's why we're one can't you see

I Stand

I stand for God and family
I stand for my daughters
    Paige Ann and Casey Lee
I stand for justice and liberty
I stand for peace and harmony
I stand for the children who go hungry
I stand for my right to be happy
And I stand for my serenity
I stand for the lady who enters the room
I stand for the stars, the sun, and the moon
I stand for Jesus, He died on the cross
I stand for freedom whatever the cost
I stand for faith, hope, and love
I stand for all things that come from above
I stand for men of any color
I stand for this, that, and the other
I stand for my brother
Yeah, I stand for my Brother
you have to stand for something
    Or you'll fall for anything
    you have to stand for something
    And nothing's free
You must open your eyes
before you can see

Outlaw

Some say I was born with a cold heart
Wearing the outlaw jacket from the start
I've been an outlaw most of my life
Stealing time from my kids and wife

They say!

I'm rotten thru and thru
What makes me do the things I do

Live by the gun life on the run
Uncut and raw, I'm the outlaw
Don't come out tonight
there's trouble in sight
Find a place to run and hide
but don't go outside

Sometimes I thought I was born to suffer
What didn't kill me has made me tougher
I don't play fair and I don't care
For heaven's sake don't make the mistake
Of turning the other cheek I'll know your week
Get out of town before the outlaw comes around

Nothing changes it remains the same
And I'm tired of this here outlaw game
Now there a new sheriff in town
I'm doing what's right laying new laws down
No longer handing out pain and hurt
I'm proud of the cross I wear under my shirt

I'm real proud of the new sheriff we got
Yeah, I really, really like him a lot

When I die, my tombstone will say:
Here lies an outlaw who found his way

Thanks Song

Written and Copyright from CD Music Hidden behind the 8 Ball 2005

I'm listening to the radio, an old country song
Thinking about my past and the things I've done wrong
I can live with the memories, so I'm moving on
God, can you tell me what took so long

Got to stay positive every day
In order to keep it, I've got to give it away
I might just get back some things I lost
Thanks to my Lord who died on the cross

All things in life can be fixed up
Like a broken-down lawn mower and a pick-up truck
It takes a little longer when it comes to broken hearts
They can't be fixed with no rebuilt parts
You can fix them up, but it just takes time
At least that's the way it was with this heart of mine

So, I'm chasing rainbows. And wishing on falling stars
Some say I've carried my dreams too far
Over the mountains and up to the stars
I bypassed the moon and made a pit stop on Mars

Not Only Women Bleed

I had the need
An addiction to feed
Now can't you see
Not only women bleed

It was a shot to the vein
So I could hear the train
I was going insane
Why can't you feel my pain

I had the need
An addiction to feed
Now can't you see
Not only women bleed

I was living a lie
I wanted to die
But could only cry
I knew I had to try
I loved my family that's why

Well now I'm alone
But I won' get stoned
All the past I own
Now I'm finally moving on

Knowing when my work is done
My King will come
So listen to the words I write
Fight a soldier's fight

Love God

As my body floated up in the sky
I seen 4 angels passing by
When I looked at my body on the ground
I seen 4 silhouettes of men
I could not make out their faces for they were looking down
So, I looked back up toward the light
I seen the face of the Lord
It felt so right
without even the time to say goodbye
I was back in my body I guess he just wanted to say hi

Someway ☆ Somehow

I can't compete with the things you do
You're a hell of a catch
But I'm not the match
Baby I can't hold a candle to you

If only I knew then
What I know now
I'd keep you in my arms
Someway somehow
When you said it was the end
It hit me then
I had lost my best friend
And we'd never be together again

Everything I've done has been to late
I must of been crazy thinking you'd wait
Drugs had me living in an altered state
Folks actually thought my life was great

If only I knew then
What I know now
I'd keep you in my Arms
Someway somehow

Cocaine and ecstasy
Had its effects on me
It caused the big wreck you see
But what did you expect of me

If only I knew then
What I know now
I'd keep you in my arms
Someway Somehow

When you said it was the end
It hit me then
I lost my best friend
And we'd never be together again
So if only I knew then
What I know now
I'd keep you in my arms
Someway Somehow

Little Things

I miss all the little things we haven't got to share
I miss all the little things like just being there
I miss all the little things like just hanging out with you
I miss all the little things like everything you do

Demons and Angels

DROWNING IN my sea of tears
Filled with all my shame and fears
For me it never disappears
Confused about the way I'm heading
I'm in too deep I must keep treading
All this confusion makes me wonder
How I let this world steal my thunder

I'm fighting a battle I can't see
Angels and demons are all around me
Deacons on my left shoulder Angels on the other
Making it hard for me to recover
I got a demon on my left
Angel on my right
The battle won't end until I see the light
My demons want to see STUMBLE
My Lord says Jimmy stay HUMBLE
Spent years lost on a side track
Today I'm taking my life back
Must not be frightened I must attack
No more 3 steps forward 5 steps back
I will never go back to where I've been
God knows I can't live like that again
Now I'm battling demons every day
My demons get weaker every time I pray…

I'm Knocking on the Door to a Heavenly Place

I lift my hands sing praise to you
I say do with me, Lord, what you wish to do
I'm praying, Lord, you'll bring me home
Not perfect in prayer so I sing you this poem

CHORUS

I'm knocking on the door to a heavenly place
Standing in the light that shines from your face
Filled with love and a delightful taste
Clean from the sin that you erased

I understand I don't have to do it alone
Because I'll never make it home on my own
So I'll go as far as my earthy body can
And wait 4 my Lord to come take my hand

Knowing that you've heard my prayer
You'll come take me the rest of the way
free from the demons that 4ever haunted me
I'll be at home with my Lord where I long to be

Good Heart / New Start

A call came only I could hear it
It came from the Holy Spirit
Like a small child I come to you
Obeying all things that are good and true
Needing someone to look up to
What you wish I will do
Take my hand and lead my way
Help me face the problems of today
Teaching me the right way to pray
Knowing what to do and what to say

Help keep me from falling
Reveal to me my true calling
Forgive me of all my sin
So that I shall be reborn again
Bring to me hope, faith, and love
strengthen me from the Lord above
Make me better equipped
To run a tighter ship
Knowing to become a true player
I must first become a true prayer
Now understanding I have a GOOD HEART
I thank you Lord for the new start

I Don't Know Everything You Need

I'm no Hollywood movie star
I don't drive NASCAR
Doing all right so far
Driving a fine car
Singing songs at the local bar
Smoke'n from the finest tree
Hang'n out just my friends and me
I may not have a college degree
But I'm working on my GED

I don't know everything you need
But I know you need a Daddy 4 our girls
For that I'm the best man in the world
Yeah 4 that I'm the best man on the world

I'm no famous football player
Ain't got no special prayer
I know life ain't always fair
And true love is rare
I'm not a prizefighter
Nor a famous writer
But I use ink and pen
To write the love letters I send

I don't know EVERYTHING you need
But I know you need a Daddy 4 our girls
For that I'm the best man in the world
Yeah 4 that I'm the best man in the world

My Intentions Were Good

Working a double shift just isn't fair
And I've taken on more than I can bear
You know I wanted to be there 4 you
But some things came up that I had to do
Cause I would have been there if only I could
I promise you honey my intentions were good

I've been swamped with paperwork and all
That's why I haven't had the time to call
So when I don't show up you need to know
There were just too many places I had to go
Cause I would have been there if only I could
I promise you honey my intentions were good

I've been told I'll be loaded down 4 days
you know as well as I do this overtime pays
So don't get frustrated hang in there honey
Soon you and I we'll be rolling in money
Cause I would have been there if only I could
I promise you honey my intentions were good

When it comes to romance I'm just a beginner
I know I promised you a candlelight dinner
But if you're waiting on me you're gonna get thinner
I'll be snowed in here 4 the rest of the winter
Cause I would have been there if only I could
I promise you honey my intentions were good

Somethings

Something's are sweet—Something's are sour
Something's last a minute—Something's last an hour
Some men are weak—Some men are tough
Some Men Are Strong—But not strong enough
Something's are never—Somethings are forever
Something's are short—Something's are long
Something's are good—Something's are wrong
Something's are fake—Something's are real
Something's you see—Something's you feel
Sometimes, some things are just no big deal

My Christmas List

Am I too old 4 the Santa Claus?
Is this Christmas a lost cause
My wish on this Christmas day
Is that your love 4 me will never go away

Spending Christmas alone is no fun
If I had a Christmas wish, baby, you'd be the one
If I could get 1 gift, I'd ask Santa 4 you
Because I love everything you say and do

Aren't no presents under my Christmas tree
Only got memories of you and me
I ain't been dance'n or shout'n with glee
Because I need you baby can't you see

Well Rudolph's nose don't shine so bright
When you're all alone on Christmas night
So I sent him packing to the North Pole
But I love you baby heart and soul

Chorus

I wish I could remember all the times that we kissed
I think I'll put it on my Christmas list
I wish I could get back all the time that I missed
So I think I'll put it on my Christmas list

Merry Christmas to all!

Where the Magic Begins (Song)

I don't know where to start
But this is where it ends
It's a place in our heart
Where the magic begins

A place where dreams start
A place where we make amends
A place in our heart
Where the magic begins

A place where love can start
A place where we keep our friends
A place in our heart
Where the magic begins

A place where forgiveness starts
A place our pain can go to mend
A place in our heart
Where the magic begins

A place where freedom starts
A place that's real not pretend
A place in our heart
Where the magic begins

It's where your soul catches fire
It's where all the madness ends
It's a place in our heart
Where the magic begins

If lost and don't know where to start
And you need freedom from your sins
There's a place in your heart
Where the magic begins

So, seek out the person you were meant to be
Set your heart and all your dreams free
If your using your heart you can only win
That my friends is where the magic begins

He Lives Upstairs

I'm real not phony
A living testimony
I was talking to my best friend
He gave me a message, he needed to send
He said to tell you!

Chorus

That he's still there, that he really cares
And he's the one who hears all our prayers
We can call him father
And he lives upstairs

I went to college
To gain some knowledge
I met a professor
Who said God had blessed her
Now she feels better
Since she found the letter
It said to tell you!

(Repeat chorus)

A boy found a bottle, halfway afloat
Inside the bottle there was a note
His life was saved
By the words that were wrote
They said to tell you!

(Repeat chorus)

What Ever Happened to Happily Ever After

I wish I was there but, I'm not
So, I have to be happy with what I've got
What I got ain't much
But, the memories of your touch
I've been looking through old pictures
To get a glimpse of your face
I've been searching for your smell, all over the place
I finally found it on my pillowcase

Well, what ever happened to happily ever after
I'm scared to write another chapter
How could love at first sight
Turn into another lonely night
For me, it couldn't have ended any worse
Because, you were sun in my universe

Without you, I'm not whole
For it was my heart that you stole
Being alone has left me terrified
I've prayed, I've cried
There is nothing I haven't tried
You were my brightest shining star
Now I wonder where you are

Something the Preacher Said

He told us how God blesses the gardens
And the flowers
But God also blesses the fields of weeds
I couldn't help second guessing
I'm not worthy of this blessing
I felt shame from somewhere inside
I couldn't hold back the tears
No matter how hard I tried
I asked myself if I deserved to live
I lived to take not to give
Then I took out my Bible read Romans
Chapter three
It said if I trust in Jesus I am set free
That God declared me not guilty of all my sin
I dropped to my knees and I thanked GOD 4 JESUS again

Daddy Don't Stop
(First Thing I Ever Wrote)

I was hidden behind an eight ball
Strung out and left 4 dead
Then two angels came to me
And this is what they said…
They said

CHORUS

Daddy, don't stop
Pick yourself up
Do your very best
You can dust yourself off
But you don't have time to rest

It's been years since that very ugly day
I'm still living so damn for away
If I'm sad and I listen hard
I can still hear my angels say!
They say:

REPEAT CHORUS

Well I missed your mom, I called her on the phone
Told her I was sorry tired of being alone
If she would 4give and let me come on home
When she finally spoke this is what she said
You never did the things you said

And you're not part of this family
So why don't you drop DEAD
That's when I remember my angels
And what they had said…

REPEAT CHORUS

Well I wish I could tell you everything was okay
But I think about my girls every second of every day
They tell me Daddy don't 4get to pray!
And remember what your angels say

They say:

REPAT CHORUS

Love Letter

How do you start a love letter
By telling her I've been in love since I met her
That it was love at first sight
And when I'm with her even the wrong feels right
That I think about her every second of the day
That I lust for her in every single way
Everything about her on the inside I adore
All the things on the outside I long to explore
The things you make me feel I have never felt
When were close my heart begins to melt
Love it is impossible to explain
Having not been with you is driving me insane
In my heart I believe we're made for each other
And being with you I've never wanted another
I guess that means our love was meant to be
That's why we'll grow old together just wait and see

God

Why did It take so long for me to come to you
It's been like a sad song in everything I say and do
There's been a whole lot of wrong the good has been mighty few
I pray you make me strong and show me the right things to do
I'm growing stronger in the Lord every single day
I'm living the right way and learning the right way to pray
Having my Lord leading me in making a better day
Like a lost sheep I come to you in all things I do
Now I don't go to sleep before I talk to you
Every day I get on my knees and ask for wisdom and strength
Knowing I will need you to keep my head clean so I can think
I love you because you complete me in every way
Knowing you are true in all things you say
If I only knew as much as you things would be okay
I know I must keep my heart with you to stay
Now when I'm feeling down and blue
I simply think of you
In Jesus's name Amen

1-800-I'm Lonely

I'm a middle-aged man still handsome and wise
Looking for a lady with love light in her eye's
Looking for a woman who's more than just a date
In need of a woman who's looking for her soul mate
Looking for a woman who looks good in heels
Must be secure in herself and know how she feels
Looking for a wife and a best friend
Must know how to cook and how to mend (not really)
Her sex drive must be off the chart
She must be strong enough to carry my heart
She must walk beside me and never behind
Must have a love just like mine (you know what I mean)
The unconditional—kind**
She looks beautiful dressed up in a skirt
Looks even better in a wet t-shirt
Doesn't live in the past only the here and now
She knows I'm not perfect but she loves me anyhow
I'm looking for my one and only
So if you're the one, the one for me
Call 1-800-I'm Lonely...

I Promise

Honey I don't blame you for being mad at me
I should 'ah picked up the kids and be home for three
"I promise" to make it up to the kids and you
But first I have some things I have to do

Honey if you can't get me on my cell
It probably broke when it fell
"I promise" I'll be coming home
If not I'll try and find a pay phone

If you think I'm selfish—I'll own it
If you think I'm a liar—I'll own it
If you say I'm not—a very good dad
I guess I'll tell you—I'll own that too
But if you think I'm happy where I'm at
Honey I got to tell ya—I don't own that

Honey Could you'd tell the kids we can't go to the show
I've got a couple places I have to go
Tell them this weekend we'll go to the zoo
"I promise" if it's the last thing I do

Honey could you tell the kids sorry about that zoo
Looks like those plans are screwed up too
Some things have come up what can I say
Just tell them "I promise" we'll go another day

Just Not Your Ordinary Man

In my dreams yeah in my dreams
I fly like superman
I know sometimes it's hard to understand
Just what I'm about and who I am
I'm just not…just not your ordinary man

I've been chased by the devil
Saved by an angel's touch
Because God loves me that much
I've made it tough on myself
But I love my Lord like everyone else
So don't quit dreaming whatever you do
God has one just for you
And He's got some more for me too
Yeah He's got some more for me too

I have imagination I've had hallucinations
I've resisted temptation on several occasions
I turn the TV on every station
What the heck I'm on vacation
And I got my PlayStation
No need for desperation
It brings on aggravation
I had a revelation I'd be the next sensation

Folks say'n slow down son
So I'm kick'n back some
You'll find me relax'n
Right here on Jackson

When I Look into My Heart

When i'm alone at night and staring into the sky
I see a shooting star I think of you and cry

Like ice cream and cake
Like beans and franks
Like nachos and cheese
We were meant to be together like all of these
When I look into my heart
I wonder why we're still apart

When I go fishing and I'm not getting a bite
I think about the times I held you tight
When I go bowling and miss my spare
I blame it on you because you weren't there
If I'm golfing and don't make my par
It's because I'm wondering where you are

So Is My Love for You

Like the rivers waters that never quit
So is my love for you

Like the sunlight that never dies
So is my love for you

Like the tree that never quits growing
So is my love for you

Like the fire that never burns down
So is my love for you

Like the universe that has no end
So is my love for you

Like a gift that never quits giving
So is my love for you

Like my love for my children
So is my love for you

unconditional

Tribute to Anna and Danny

No one was ready 4 Anna to die
They wonder how they wonder why
Well Big Mo called it from the start
Anna Nichole died of a broken heart
Imagine losing a child of your own
How hard it would be to keep moving on
Press and paparazzi won't leave you alone
With all their questions about methadone
Rumors from people you've known
In the end we all reap what we've sown
Anna Nichole just wanted to go home
I know if I had lost a child of my own
I would also feel like dying
I could not go on I'm not lying
Never lost a child but I've lost a best friend
I remember asking God to take me then
I know it was wrong and probably a sin
Dying's not the answer when you suffer a loss
But Anna needed Danny and would pay the cost
They're together now but in a much better place
God has put a smile back on Anna's face
The real loser here is her baby Danny Lee
A brother and mother she'll never see
If Robert's not the daddy let's find out who is
Danny Lee should most certainly be his
A father's love is equal to none
Wouldn't that make him the perfect one
It doesn't take a rocket scientist to see

TOGETHER'S WHERE ANNA AND DANNY WERE MEANT TO BE
LORD LET ME LIE BY MY DANNY TODAY
YOU KNOW I WOULDN'T HAVE IT ANY OTHER WAY

Written in Dallas, Texas, 2007, In memory of Anna Nicole

Baby Don't Cry

Baby don't cry, don't cry I'll tell you why
Daddy's coming home soon to be with you
We'll do all the things daddies and daughters do
I'll take you to the park and maybe the zoo
We'll stop by Mikey Dee's and have a french fry too
We'll go on walks and just play outside
I'll count to ten and you'll run and hide
You'll tell me silly jokes I'll sing you a song
If I have to go to work you can tag along
I'll take pictures at your school play
I'll make movies when you have field day
I'll capture the smile on your face
When you cross the finish line in first place
We'll rent a big room one that's really cool
Spend the whole day just swimming in the pool
We'll eat and crash out in front of the TV
I'll look at you and you'll look at me
And we'll know we're right where we should be
We'll go to the movies drink popcorn and eat soda
We'll sing the songs daddy wrote ya
I'll hug you and kiss you and I'll just hold ya
Yeah' we'll do all the things daddy told ya
Daddy's coming home soon to be with you
We'll do all the things daddies and daughters do

I'm Thinking I Love You

I WAS THINKING THAT YOU WERE THINKING ABOUT ME YOU WERE THINKING THAT I WAS THINKING ABOUT YOU I WAS THINKING I LOVE YOU

I WAS DREAMING THAT YOU WERE DREAMING ABOUT ME YOU WERE DREAMING THAT I WAS DREAMING ABOUT YOU I WAS DREAMING THAT I LOVE YOU

I HAD A VISION THAT YOU HAD A VISION ABOUT ME YOU HAD A VISION THAT I HAD A VISION ABOUT YOU I WAS HAVING A VISION THAT I LOVE YOU

I WAS PRAYING THAT YOU WERE PRAYING ABOUT ME YOU WERE PRAYING THAT I WAS PRAYING ABOUT YOU I WAS PRAYING THAT YOU LOVED ME TOO

Do as I Say Not as I Do

Do as I say not as I do
I'm telling you this cause I love you
I'm your dad and I made a lot of mistakes
But I know you have what it takes

I want to teach you the right way
It's not always about what you say
It's about how you say it
Don't just pray about it
be about it

I told you, you could be
Anything you wanted to be
Then you started bouncing on that bed
I told you to quit, then you said

Daddy, you said I could do
Anything I wanted to
I said
You could be anything you wanna be
she looked at me and said
Daddy, I wanna be
Bouncing on that bed

Opp's Hold On

On my way now to the purple cow
Yeah it's where I want to be
My best friend Tater he'll be there waiting on me
That bars our second home—opp's hold on
I'd better hurry Tater don't like drinking alone

Then we will talk about the past—how nothing last
We'll talk about cars how we love to drive them fast
I'll talk about my daughters he'll talk about his son
"Opp's hold on" here comes a cold one

He'll talk about a truck and a girl with no name
We'll talk about the good ol' days and my golf game
We'll talk about work—we will talk about fun
"Opp's hold on" here comes a cold one

I'll talk about being up and how I fell
We'll talk about heaven and we'll talk about hell
We'll talk about life and the things we've done
"Opp's hold on" here comes a cold one

We'll talk about laws and talk about guns
I'll talk about the times I carried one
We'll talk about the days we were on the run
"Opp's hold on" here comes a cold one

Hide and Seek

JIMMY, JIMMY, CAN YOU COME OUT AND PLAY
WE'RE PLAYING HIDE AND SEEK WE'LL LOOK FOR YOU TODAY
JIMMY, JIMMY, CAN YOU COME ON IN!
WE'VE LOOKED BUT WE CAN'T FIND WHERE YOUR HIDE'N
HOW ABOUT WE COUNT TO TEN…

1-2-3-4-5-6-7-8-9 AND 10 LOOK OUT, JIMMY, HERE WE COME AGAIN

WHO'S THAT MAN BEHIND THE MASK HIDING ALL HIS FEARS
WHO'S THE MAN THAT HIDES SO NO ONE CAN SEE HIS TEARS
IT'S TIME TO OPEN UP AND SHOW THEM WHO YOU ARE
BECAUSE EVEN THE LORD KNOWS YOU HAVE COME WAY TO FAR
SO COME OUT, COME OUT! ARE YOU IN THERE
IT'S TIME TO QUIT PRETENDING, LIKE YOU DON'T EVEN CARE

OLLIE, OLLIE ODDSON, FREE, YOU CAN COME ON IN
WE'VE GIVEN UP WE CAN'T FIND YOU AGAIN
WE LOOKED HERE WE LOOKED THERE
STILL CAN'T FIND YOU ANYWHERE
NOW WE'RE QUIT'N, THIS GAME JUST NEVER SEEMS FAIR
AND YOU NEVER LET US FIND YOU
NO MATTER WHAT WE DO…

Little Things That Heaven Brings

Casey and Paige, I can remember when you were
Both little things...I thank God for the little things
Little things that heaven brings
I realize little things aren't so little anymore
Little things are the things you love
But can't buy in a store
Like coming home and seeing your daughter
Waiting at the door
Baby girls aren't so little all grown up now
Still love their daddy sometimes I don't know how
When I was young I took little things 4 granted
I'm older now still don't understand it
Yes, it's the little things I miss most in life
Like a hug from my kids or a kiss from my wife

Time Stolen

Worst thing about not being with you
Is that I'll miss the first things that you do
Like all the cute little faces you make
Or watching the first steps you take

I will miss the first words you say
Or being there 4 your birthday
Even though I'm not there to watch you grow
I love you baby girl from head to toe

There's a lot of things I can't stand
Like not being able to hold your hand
Or holding you in my arms to steal a kiss
It's the memories stole that I will miss

Sometimes life just doesn't seem fair
Wanted you to know I wish I was there
When someone mentions the word love
You'll be the one i'm thinking of

Leave My Dreams Alone

Why do I feel like I am swimming upstream
With a broken heart and a pipe dream
Stuck upstream without a paddle
My love for you has been a burr in my saddle
It's a feeling that won't go away
No matter how hard I try—or how much I pray
Everything I see is a reminder to me
Of how the way things used to be
Shoot me dead and set me free
Or come back to bed and made sweet love to me
Reaching for you is like reaching for the stars
Well baby I'm out there on Mars
Well I wish you would leave my dreams alone
There all I have left to call my own
Because you took my baby girls and left that day
Then you ripped out my heart and walked away
You were the only thing left in life that seemed real
But you walked out on me like I was no big deal
You never gave a thought about how I would feel
But don't you worry honey it was no big deal

Happy Song

I'm happy when the cardinals win the pennant
Watching the pistons win it
Or when the lions are even in it!
My girls say they love me and I know they meant it
Purple sunsets my eyes love to see
Hang'n out with people I know love me
Like Paige Ann and Casey Lee
Or going to visit little Tater's and Micky Dee's
Watching late night shows on TV
Or just being the person God wants me to be
I love watching my cardinals play ball
Jimmy ball game robbing a home run at the wall
Then watch Puhols touch them all
Or watching a Wainwright roundhouse curveball
I just wrote this to tell you get back up if you fall

Reminisce List

BEING ALONE SURE GIVES YOU TIME TO REMINISCE
ABOUT ALL THE THINGS YOU REALLY MISS
SO WHILE I'M SITTING HERE I THINK I'LL MAKE A LIST
NUMBER 1 WOULD BE THE FIRST TIME WE EVER KISSED
NUMBER ONE WAS EASY AND SO IS NUMBER TWO
IT HAS TO BE THE FIRST TIME THAT I MADE LOVE TO YOU
I HAD TO PUT A LITTLE THOUGHT INTO NUMBER THREE
LET'S JUST SAY IT'S THOSE LITTLE THINGS THAT YOU DO 4 ME
THEN OF COURSE THERE'S MY LUCKY NUMBER 4
SO I'M FEELING LUCKY WHEN YOUR CLOTHES HIT THE FLOOR
WHAT CAN I SAY ABOUT NUMBER FIVE
IT HAS TO BE THE WAY YOU MAKE MY SOUL FEEL SO ALIVE
MY PERSONAL FAVORITE MIGHT BE NUMBER SIX
LIKE WHEN WE'RE TOGETHER AND THERE'S NOTHING LEFT TO FIX
HOW ABOUT THIS FOR NUMBER SEVEN
BEING IN YOUR ARMS IS AS CLOSE AS I'VE BEEN TO HEAVEN
DIDN'T HAVE TO THINK ABOUT MY NUMBER EIGHT
IT'S THE NIGHTS WE SPENT TOGETHER THEY WERE GREAT
HERE'S NUMBER NINE IF YOU WANT I'LL PUT IT ON A SIGN
IT'S BECAUSE I LOVE YOU AND YOU ARE MINE
EVEN THOUGH THE LIST GOES ON I'LL END AT NUMBER TEN
IT'S NO MATTER HOW MANY TIMES WE MAKE LOVE
I CAN'T WAIT
TO DO IT AGAIN...

Rock Bottom

I was living the nightmares
That I dreamed
But I didn't care so it seemed
Even though my heart screamed
                              Yeah

Rock bottom ain't so far away
Maybe I'll find him today
I've been doing wrong like I'm supposed to
What's taken so long to find you
Maybe I'm too sick to know I got'um
Has anyone seen my rock bottom
Please let me know if you spot'um

I've been going to all the wrong places
Sharing the pain I see on their faces
Looking deep into my wounds
Maybe I'll find him in a tear
Maybe he'll just appear
In my reflection in the mirror

Rock bottom ain't so far away
Maybe I'll find him today

Thought Love Was Forever

I thought love was forever
Like my love for you
But I was wrong it only last
As long as you want it to

I prayed our love would never end
Nothing last forever not since way back when
But if our love is lost
Could we at least be friends

I thought love would see us through
Like my love for you
But I was wrong it only last
As long as you want it too

I thought love was something that grew
Like my love for you
But I was wrong it only last
As long as you want it too

I thought our love was true
Like my love for you
But I was wrong it only last as long
As long as you want it too

Trapped in My Mind

When I'm sad or broken hearted
I remember how and why it started
Feeling empty and all alone
No one to talk to
Not even on the phone
It left an empty feeling I can't explain
It hurt's more than physical pain
Trapped in a storm wind more than strong
Change is hard but not wrong
So beat down I drop to my knees
I said Lord you are my light and my life
Would you take control please
The storm has finally passed and I'll survive
Jesus is my savior and I'm still alive

Left a Note

They found my body lying dead
There was a gun found by my head
They found a note by my bed
This is what it said

It said I couldn't take it no more
That just living had became a chore
I messed up a long time back
Way before the ice and crack
Losing my family was more than I could take
It hurt me worse than death 4 heaven's sake
Too much guilt and all the shame
With only myself to blame
I tried to find myself but it had been too long
I prayed 4 forgiveness 4 the things I'd done wrong
I wish I could have just said no
It never happened so it was time to go
What was bad from the start
I was a good man in my heart of hearts

Destiny

SINCE I SENT YOU THAT FRIEND REQUEST
IT'S BEEN ME THAT WAS BLESSED
OUT OF ALL MY FRIENDS YOU ARE THE BEST
MORE BEAUTIFUL AND KIND THAN ALL THE REST
YOU HAVE MADE ME BELIEVE IN LOVE AGAIN
SO IF YOU LOVE ME OR JUST WANT A FRIEND
NOW I BELIEVE JUST MAYBE THERE IS SOMEONE 4 ME
4 THE FIRST TIME MY HEART IS OPEN AND FREE
IT'S A LONG SHOT BUT I HOPE YOU FEEL THE SAME 4 ME
I KNOW YOU MAY NOT AGREE
BUT IF WE DON'T TRY WE'LL NEVER SEE
SO HOLD ON TIGHT 4 A WILD AND CRAZY RIDE
DON'T WORRY YOU'LL BE RIGHT HERE BY MV SIDE
I'M NOT SURE IF I'VE EVER GIVEN MY HEART AWAY
IT'S BEEN BROKEN BUT SUDDENLY SEEMS OKAY
I'M HOPING YOU WILL FEEL THE SAME ONE DAY
4 THIS I BEND AT THE KNEES AND PRAY
WE DON'T HAVE 4EVER. BUT WHAT DO YOU SAY
GOD DID BRING US TOGETHER IN A SPECIAL WAY
YOU TOUCHED MY LIFE LIKE NO ONE BEFORE
MY HEART FEELS NEW LIKE ONE FRESH FROM A STORE
TO HUG YOU AND KISS YOUR NECK I CAN'T WAIT
4 THIS WILL BE AN UNFORGETTABLE DATE
THE DAY GOD LET ME HOLD MY SOUL MATE
THIS MEANS TO ME...I WAS RIGHT ABOUT DESTINY

Roam'n

I've been roam'n and roam'n, roam'n around
I'm a small country boy lost in a big city town
Looking for a place I can settle down
I'm a small country boy lost in a big city town

I've been roam'n and roam'n, roam'n around
I'm a small country boy lost in a big city town
Looking for a woman I ain't found
I'm a small country boy lost in a big city town

I've been roam'n and roam'n, roam'n around
I'm a small country boy lost in a big city town
You should have seen me coming I've covered some ground
I'm a small country boy lost in a big city town

I've been roam'n and roam'n, roam'n around
I'm a small country boy lost in a big city town
Walking for days I'm tired and rundown
I'm a small country boy lost in a big city town

I've been roam'n and roam'n, roam'n around
I'm a small country boy lost in a big city town
I've been looking for something I ain't found
I'm a small country boy lost in a big city town

Enlightenment

THERE'LL BE NO MORE POEMS OR LOVE LETTERS
NO MORE SONGS TO MAKE YOU FEEL BETTER
THE HOLE IN MY HEART IS PATCHED AND MENDED
I'M MOVE'N ON JUST LIKE GOD INTENDED
THIS IS THE HARDEST THING I'VE EVER DONE
WHEN IT CAME TO LOVE YOU WERE THE ONE
I'M WORKING HARD TO ANSWER THE CALL
NOW I DON'T USE DRUGS AND ALCOHOL
WHEN LOVE IS LOST WE CAN STILL BE FRIENDS
YEAH THIS IS WHERE THE MAGIC BEGINS
I'M STILL DREAM'N MY DREAMS OUT LOUD
MY HEADS STILL TEN FEET ABOVE THE CLOUDS
I HAVEN'T CHANGED MUCH IN ALL THESE YEARS
I DON'T USE DRUGS TO HIDE MY FEARS
TODAY I ONLY WANT WHAT'S REAL
ANYTHING ELSE IS NO BIG DEAL
I ONLY WANT WHAT I CAN TOUCH AND FEEL
ANYTHING ELSE IS NO BIG DEAL

In This Crazy Life of Mine

Sometimes I wonder what you're doing up there
Or if you will even answer my next prayer
When it comes it will be in your perfect time
In this crazy life of mine
With eyes open wide you can see all things
Ears to hear a bird make a song while he sings
If your eyes are closed so is your mind
In this crazy life of mine
Put yourself in their shoes before you destroy
You will then know how it feels to be treated as a toy
Prepare in life about what you know is real
Empathy and feeling should be part of the deal
Focus on things that you can touch and feel
Why does it feel like I must throw up a sign
In this crazy life of mine
Don't let the past slow you down
Or push your face in the ground
Searching for things I need to find
In this crazy life of mine
Give me a special place for my heart to be
Like on the ballfields where I felt free
I want to be where my soul will shine
Or simply go to unwind
From this crazy life of mine

That's How Daddy's Love

More than all grains of sand on the beach
Further than the stars or man can reach
Deeper than the ocean
More powerful than the rivers current
Yeah that's how daddy's love
Yeah that's how daddy's love
A daddy always has an unconditional love
It was given to him by the Man above
They go crazy when their babies cry
They love their kids only God knows why
Yeah that's how daddy's love
Yeah that's how daddy's love
For heaven's sake it is never fake
A daddy's love is unmistakable
Therefore unescapable
Most definitely unbreakable
For this is all they're capable
Yeah that's how daddy's love
Yeah that's how daddy's love

The Best of You

The best of you is not me
You I could never be
I want you to know
Can't you see
I know the world is not so free
It took all the peace and harmony
Gave me pain and agony
Never been a better friend to me
Can't you see

The best of you is not me
You I could never be
Dreams are what set us free
It was you that made me see
We didn't know
That the cost would be
All the time we lost you see
The most precious thing of mine
Is the memories of our time

The best of you is not me
You I could never be
Loneliness is being without you
What do you want me to do
With you on my mind
My brother all the time
I remember the night
You turned out the light
Though you gave up a fight
Doesn't make it feel right

Two Lost Souls

WHERE TWO LOST SOULS ON THE CRUISE SHIP LONELINESS
THERE TO ASK GOD WHY THEY'RE FEELING EMPTINESS
OUT ON THE DECK TO WATCH THE SUN RISE
GOD REACHES OUT WHEN HE HEARS THEIR CRIES
THEY FEEL GOD'S LOVE AND THE EMPTINESS SUBSIDES
BY GOD'S GRACE THEY SEE A PURPLE SUNSET
BUT THEY HAVEN'T MET YET
LATER IN NIGHT THE LOST SOULS BOTH WITNESS A SHOOTING STAR
THE LOST SOULS SEE THIS AS A MESSAGE AND BEGIN TO LOVE WHO
THEY ARE
THE NEXT MORNING FEELING BORN AGAIN LIKE A WEIGHT HAS BEEN
LIFTED
WITH GOD BACK IN THERE LIFE THEY FEEL GIFTED
THAT AFTERNOON UP ON THE DECK THEY FEEL THE RHYTHM OF THE
SEA
THEN THANK GOD 4 THE THINGS THAT HE HAS GIVEN THEM TO FEEL
AND SEE
NOW THERE IN GOD'S CARE AND EXACTLY WHERE THEY SHOULD BE
THE SOULS REALIZE THAT ALL THE BEST THINGS IN LIFE ARE FREE...

By the way, these two souls are together now for eternity.

Nothing's Better Than You

To my surprise
When I looked into her eyes
What a beautiful smile
She returned to me
I'm gonna love her
You just wait and see

My mind is doing time
Since I don't know when
Locked out of sleep
Will this ever end

Spend my nights thinking of you
And the things that you do
Love is perfect can't you see
The way our love was meant to be

Everything is better than something
Something is better than nothing
But baby

Ain't nothing better than you
Yeah ain't nothing better than you...

About A Dream

When I fly I fly like Jesus would
With my arms open wide
And my head held high
My hair hangs down
On my white tail suit

And there's glow about me
That's all you need to know
About me

When I fly like Jesus would
My eyes shine blue
I'm wearing sandles 4 shoes
There's a smile on my face
Put there by heavenly place

And there's a glow about me
That's all you need to know
About me

About the Author

Jimmy was born in 1958 in Grand Rapids, Michigan. He was the middle child of a family of five. He grew up in a family where abuse and fighting between his parents seemed normal, as was the constant abuse that he suffered mostly when his parents were drunk. Jimmy turned to sports as a way out at an early age. It's where he felt free, and he loved it. Jimmy continued to play baseball and softball at a high level until he was forty-three years old. He learned about God and Jesus at an early age as he rode the bus to Sunday school and still remembers the first Bible verse he memorized at the age of eight: John 3:16.

At the age of seven, he was saved by an angel from drowning, which only enlightened his faith and love for Jesus. By the time Jimmy was a teenager, he had seen the ugly part of the world as he would break his neck playing football in his senior year in high school and, a year later, lose his best friend in a head-on collision where Jimmy was hit driver to driver. He was going thirty-five, and the driver in the other car was traveling at seventy. Jimmy broke his back, crushed his heel through the floorboard, and broke his legs.

Later in life, Jimmy found himself with a bad addiction to cocaine, which would challenge his faith and the love of his daughters—even life itself. By the age of forty-three, Jimmy had lost everything he loved. It was in a prison rehab facility in 2005 where Jimmy again found Jesus, and it brought with it a passion for writing song and poetry.

CPSIA information can be obtained
at www.ICGtesting.com
Printed in the USA
BVHW090013060821
613729BV00003B/461